WORKBOOK

For

Third-Heaven Authority

Discover How To Pray from Heaven's Perspective

[A Guide to Implementing Mike Thompson's Book]

Kelly Press

Table of Content

How To Use This Workbook

This workbook provides you with the chance to investigate a variety of aspects of your life, identify areas in need of improvement, and observe your advancement. It has a compilation of essential topics, questions to stimulate contemplation, and learning review questions to gauge your progression.

To ensure you stay on track and make progress, it's advised that you establish a timeline for completing the workbook. Set aside specific periods to work through the prompts and learning review questions. This will help you maintain your momentum and ensure you make steady progress.

The workbook commences with a short recap of the main book, acquainting you with the topic discussed in the title. This approach is highly beneficial for obtaining a deeper understanding of the content covered in the workbook, as well as identifying the areas that require the most attention.

The key lessons and the action prompts provided in this workbook aim to inspire contemplation on various facets of your life. You need not respond to all of them simultaneously and may revisit them later. They serve as a base for your self-reflection and personal exploration.

Once you complete the activities in this workbook, you can assess your progress by answering self-assessment questions. The purpose of these questions is to prompt you to reflect on your learning and identify which areas you need to focus on more. Armed with this knowledge, you can devise effective strategies to enhance your comprehension of the material.

Feel free to spend enough time on the prompts and self-assessment questions. You do not need to finish them in one go. You can take a pause and come back to them later. The most significant thing is to be truthful to yourself and to give careful thought to your responses.

Good luck!

Kelly Press

Overview

Mike Thompson's book "Third-Heaven Authority" is a spiritual and theological work. The book delves into the biblical notion of the "third heaven" and how believers might get access to it in order to experience greater power and influence in their life.

The book is split into chapters, each of which focuses on a distinct facet of the third heaven. Thompson presents the notion of the third heaven and how it pertains to spiritual authority in the opening chapter. The third heaven, he continues, is a region beyond the physical and spiritual realms where Christians can access God's power and dominion.

The next chapters dive into many features of the third heaven, such as God's throne chamber, the heavenly world, and the power of Jesus' blood. Thompson also highlights the significance of living a holy and blameless life, as well as how believers might gain entry to the third heaven via prayer and worship.

The importance of spiritual warfare is one of the book's main topics. According to Thompson, the third heaven is a battleground where believers must combat spiritual forces of darkness. To combat these influences, he highlights the need of understanding one's identity in Christ and having a firm trust in God.

Thompson provides personal experiences and testimony throughout the book about how reaching the third heaven has impacted his own life and ministry. He also offers exercises and prayers that readers may employ to help them on their own spiritual path.

"Third-Heaven Authority" is a thought-provoking and compelling book that pushes readers to strengthen their spiritual walk and access God's power and authority. Thompson's writing style is exciting and simple, making the book accessible to both new and seasoned Christians.

My First Visit to the Third Heaven

Key Lessons

1. The third heaven is a real and tangible place where believers can access the presence and power of God.

2. The importance of humility and surrender in approaching the throne of God, recognizing that we cannot earn or deserve His grace.

3. The power of worship and praise in accessing the third heaven and experiencing the glory of God.

4. The significance of spiritual warfare and recognizing that the third heaven is a battleground where we must fight against spiritual forces of darkness.

5. The importance of personal holiness and obedience to God in accessing and experiencing the fullness of His power and authority.

Action Prompts

Have you ever experienced a visitation or encounter with God that transformed your understanding of His presence and power?

_____

_____

_____

_____

_____

_____

_____

_____

_____

_____

_____

_____

_____

How do you approach God in prayer and worship? Are you willing to humble yourself and surrender your will to His?

_____

_____

_____

_____

_____

_____

_____

_____

_____

_____

_____

_____

_____

_____

_____

What role does praise and worship play in your spiritual life? How do you cultivate a heart of worship and adoration towards God?

_____

_____

_____

_____

_____

_____

_____

_____

_____

_____

_____

_____

_____

_____

_____

Do you recognize the reality of spiritual warfare and the need to fight against spiritual forces of darkness? How do you arm yourself with the spiritual weapons of God?

_____

_____

_____

_____

_____

_____

_____

_____

_____

_____

_____

_____

_____

_____

How does your personal holiness and obedience to God impact your ability to access and experience the power and authority of the third heaven?

_____

_____

_____

_____

_____

_____

_____

_____

_____

_____

_____

_____

_____

_____

_____

Are you willing to take risks and step out in faith to access the third heaven and experience the fullness of God's power and authority in your life?

_____

_____

_____

_____

_____

_____

_____

_____

_____

_____

_____

_____

_____

_____

How can you cultivate a deeper hunger and thirst for the presence of God and the power of the third heaven in your spiritual walk?

_____

_____

_____

_____

_____

_____

_____

_____

_____

_____

_____

_____

A View From Heaven

Key Lessons

1. There is a third heaven that exists beyond the physical and spiritual realms that believers can access through faith in Jesus Christ, and it is a place of great power and authority.

2. The third heaven is a realm of intense light and glory, and it is filled with angelic beings and the presence of God.

3. In the third heaven, believers can receive revelations and insights that can transform their lives and ministries.

4. The third heaven is also a place of great warfare, and believers must be equipped with spiritual armor and weapons to fight against spiritual forces of darkness.

5. Accessing the third heaven requires faith, purity, and a heart that is fully surrendered to God.

Action Prompts

Have you ever considered the existence of a third heaven beyond the physical and spiritual realms?

_____

_____

_____

_____

_____

_____

_____

_____

_____

_____

_____

_____

_____

_____

How might accessing the power and authority of the third heaven transform your life and ministry?

_____

_____

_____

_____

_____

_____

_____

_____

_____

_____

_____

_____

_____

_____

_____

How can you deepen your faith in Jesus Christ in order to access the third heaven more fully?

_____

_____

_____

_____

_____

_____

_____

_____

_____

_____

_____

_____

_____

_____

_____

Are there areas of impurity or unrighteousness in your life that may hinder your ability to access the third heaven?

_____

_____

_____

_____

_____

_____

_____

_____

_____

_____

_____

_____

How can you better equip yourself with spiritual armor and weapons to fight against spiritual warfare?

_____

_____

_____

_____

_____

_____

_____

_____

_____

_____

_____

_____

_____

_____

_____

Are there revelations or insights that you are seeking from God that can only be received through accessing the third heaven?

_____

_____

_____

_____

_____

_____

_____

_____

_____

_____

_____

_____

_____

_____

_____

How can you cultivate a heart that is fully surrendered to God in order to access the fullness of the third heaven?

_____

_____

_____

_____

_____

_____

_____

_____

_____

_____

_____

_____

_____

_____

The Third-Heaven Epistle

Key Lessons

1. The third heaven is a realm beyond the natural and spiritual realms, where believers can access the power and authority of God to overcome spiritual battles.

2. Believers can access the third heaven through prayer, worship, and living a holy and righteous life.

3. Knowing one's identity in Christ is essential for spiritual warfare and accessing the third heaven.

4. The blood of Jesus is a powerful tool for overcoming the attacks of the enemy and accessing the third heaven.

5. Believers must use their spiritual gifts and authority to advance the Kingdom of God and bring glory to Him.

Action Prompts

How can you deepen your prayer and worship life to better access the third heaven?

_____

_____

_____

_____

_____

_____

_____

_____

_____

_____

_____

_____

_____

_____

What steps can you take to live a more holy and righteous life?

_____

_____

_____

_____

_____

_____

_____

_____

_____

_____

_____

_____

_____

_____

_____

What does knowing your identity in Christ mean to you,
and how can you apply it to your spiritual warfare?

_____

_____

_____

_____

_____

_____

_____

_____

_____

_____

_____

_____

_____

_____

How can you use the blood of Jesus to overcome the attacks of the enemy and access the third heaven?

_____

_____

_____

_____

_____

_____

_____

_____

_____

_____

_____

_____

How can you use your spiritual gifts and authority to advance the Kingdom of God in your daily life?

_____

_____

_____

_____

_____

_____

_____

_____

_____

_____

_____

_____

_____

_____

_____

What obstacles are hindering you from accessing the third heaven, and how can you overcome them?

_____

_____

_____

_____

_____

_____

_____

_____

_____

_____

_____

_____

_____

_____

What can you do to continue growing in your spiritual journey and accessing the power and authority of God in your life?

_____

_____

_____

_____

_____

_____

_____

_____

_____

_____

_____

_____

_____

_____

Authority on Earth as in Heaven

Key Lessons

1. Believers have been given authority on earth as in heaven through the power of the Holy Spirit.

2. This authority is not based on our own strength or merit, but on the finished work of Jesus Christ.

3. To exercise this authority, we must have a revelation of our identity in Christ and walk in obedience to His Word.

4. Our authority is not just for our own benefit, but to bring the kingdom of God to the earth and advance His purposes.

5. The devil and his forces will resist us as we exercise our authority, but we have the power to overcome them through the name of Jesus and the blood of the Lamb.

Action Prompts

Do you believe that you have been given authority on earth as in heaven as a believer? Why or why not?

_____

_____

_____

_____

_____

_____

_____

_____

_____

_____

_____

_____

_____

How does your understanding of your identity in Christ impact your ability to exercise your authority?

_____

_____

_____

_____

_____

_____

_____

_____

_____

_____

_____

_____

_____

_____

_____

In what ways have you seen the kingdom of God advanced through your exercise of authority?

_____

_____

_____

_____

_____

_____

_____

_____

_____

_____

_____

_____

_____

_____

What are some practical ways you can walk in greater obedience to God's Word to exercise your authority more effectively?

_____

_____

_____

_____

_____

_____

_____

_____

_____

_____

_____

_____

_____

_____

How do you respond when you face resistance from the enemy as you exercise your authority? What can you do to overcome this resistance?

_____

_____

_____

_____

_____

_____

_____

_____

_____

_____

_____

_____

_____

_____

_____

Are there areas in your life where you have not been exercising your authority as you should? How can you change this?

_____

_____

_____

_____

_____

_____

_____

_____

_____

_____

_____

_____

_____

_____

How can you partner with other believers to exercise
your authority and advance the kingdom of God
together?

_____

_____

_____

_____

_____

_____

_____

_____

_____

_____

_____

_____

_____

_____

_____

Levels of Spiritual Influence

Key Lessons

1. We all have a sphere of influence in the spiritual realm, and the level of our influence is determined by our level of spiritual maturity and authority.

2. To increase our level of influence, we must first submit ourselves to God and allow Him to purify and transform us.

3. The use of our spiritual authority should always be aligned with God's will and purposes, rather than our own desires.

4. Our level of influence can be hindered by unforgiveness and bitterness, which can create blockages in our spiritual life.

5. As we grow in spiritual maturity and authority, we must also be mindful of the responsibility that comes with greater influence and use it for the glory of God.

Action Prompts

What is the current level of your spiritual influence, and how has it changed over time?

_____

_____

_____

_____

_____

_____

_____

_____

_____

_____

_____

_____

_____

In what ways have you submitted yourself to God and allowed Him to transform you?

_____

_____

_____

_____

_____

_____

_____

_____

_____

_____

_____

_____

_____

_____

Can you think of a time when you used your spiritual authority for your own desires rather than God's will? How did that turn out?

_____

_____

_____

_____

_____

_____

_____

_____

_____

_____

_____

_____

_____

_____

Have you ever struggled with unforgiveness or
bitterness? How has that affected your spiritual life and
level of influence?

_____

_____

_____

_____

_____

_____

_____

_____

_____

_____

_____

_____

_____

What is one way you can use your spiritual influence to
bring glory to God?

_____

_____

_____

_____

_____

_____

_____

_____

_____

_____

_____

_____

_____

Who are some people in your sphere of influence that you can mentor or disciple in their spiritual walk?

_____

_____

_____

_____

_____

_____

_____

_____

_____

_____

_____

_____

_____

_____

How can you continue to grow in spiritual maturity and
authority, and what steps can you take to achieve that
growth?

_____

_____

_____

_____

_____

_____

_____

_____

_____

_____

_____

_____

_____

Walking in Heavenly Authority

Key Lessons

1. You have been given authority as a believer: Thompson explains that as believers, we have been given authority through Christ to overcome spiritual forces of darkness and access the power of God.

2. You must understand your identity in Christ: Understanding our identity in Christ is crucial to walking in heavenly authority and accessing the power of the third heaven.

3. You must walk in holiness: Walking in holiness and righteousness is essential to accessing the power and authority of God and living a victorious life.

4. You must renew your mind: Renewing our minds through the Word of God is key to transforming our thinking and accessing the power of the third heaven.

5. You must persevere in faith: Persevering in faith and not giving up in the face of spiritual warfare is essential to walking in heavenly authority and accessing the power of God.

Action Prompts

How have you been using the authority given to you as a believer?

_____

_____

_____

_____

_____

_____

_____

_____

_____

_____

_____

_____

_____

Do you truly understand your identity in Christ? If not, what steps can you take to gain a deeper understanding?

_____

_____

_____

_____

_____

_____

_____

_____

_____

_____

_____

_____

_____

_____

How committed are you to walking in holiness and righteousness?

_____

_____

_____

_____

_____

_____

_____

_____

_____

_____

_____

_____

_____

_____

Are you consistently renewing your mind through the Word of God? If not, what changes can you make to prioritize this practice?

_____

_____

_____

_____

_____

_____

_____

_____

_____

_____

_____

_____

_____

_____

How do you respond to spiritual warfare? Do you give up easily or persevere in faith?

_____

_____

_____

_____

_____

_____

_____

_____

_____

_____

_____

_____

_____

_____

_____

What areas of your life do you need to surrender to God in order to access greater levels of heavenly authority?

_____

_____

_____

_____

_____

_____

_____

_____

_____

_____

_____

_____

_____

_____

In what ways can you practically apply the lessons from this chapter in your daily life and walk with God?

_____

_____

_____

_____

_____

_____

_____

_____

_____

_____

_____

_____

_____

_____

Five Ways Satan Questions Your Authority

Key Lessons

1. Satan challenges your identity in Christ to undermine your authority - Satan tries to get you to question who you are in Christ and your position as a child of God, in order to weaken your authority and power in spiritual warfare.

2. Satan will question the legitimacy of your spiritual experiences to discredit your authority - Satan may try to make you doubt or question the validity of your spiritual experiences, such as hearing God's voice, receiving visions or dreams, or experiencing miracles, in order to make you feel like you don't have the authority to share them with others.

3. Satan tries to use your past mistakes and sins to rob you of your authority - Satan will remind you of your past mistakes and sins, trying to make you feel unworthy or disqualified to operate in spiritual authority.

4. Satan will use fear to intimidate you and make you question your authority - Satan may try to use fear

and intimidation to make you doubt your authority and power, especially when facing spiritual attacks or opposition.

5. Satan will try to make you believe you need more knowledge or experience to have authority - Satan may try to make you feel like you need more knowledge or experience to operate in spiritual authority, leading you to believe that you are not ready or qualified to confront spiritual warfare or opposition.

Action Prompts

Have you ever experienced any of these ways Satan tries to question your authority?

_____

_____

_____

_____

_____

_____

_____

_____

_____

_____

_____

_____

_____

How do you usually respond when Satan tries to make you doubt your identity in Christ?

_____

_____

_____

_____

_____

_____

_____

_____

_____

_____

_____

_____

_____

_____

_____

What steps do you take to combat fear and intimidation from the enemy?

_____

_____

_____

_____

_____

_____

_____

_____

_____

_____

_____

_____

_____

_____

_____

How do you guard against believing you need more knowledge or experience to operate in spiritual authority?

_____

_____

_____

_____

_____

_____

_____

_____

_____

_____

_____

_____

_____

Have past mistakes or sins ever made you feel unworthy or disqualified to operate in spiritual authority?

_____

_____

_____

_____

_____

_____

_____

_____

_____

_____

_____

_____

_____

_____

_____

How do you discern the validity of your spiritual experiences when Satan tries to make you doubt them?

_____

_____

_____

_____

_____

_____

_____

_____

_____

_____

_____

_____

_____

_____

What scriptures or truths do you cling to when facing spiritual attacks or opposition?

_____

_____

_____

_____

_____

_____

_____

_____

_____

_____

_____

_____

_____

_____

Hosting God's Presence

Key Lessons

1. Hosting God's presence requires a heart of surrender and obedience to His will, as well as a lifestyle of holiness and righteousness.

2. When God's presence is hosted, there is a tangible manifestation of His power and glory that can transform lives and environments.

3. Hosting God's presence requires intentional effort, including setting aside time for prayer, worship, and reading His Word.

4. When God's presence is hosted, it can bring both blessings and challenges, as the power of God exposes and purges any impurities or sin in the host's life.

5. Hosting God's presence is not limited to specific locations or events, but can be experienced in any moment and any place where believers seek and invite His presence.

Action Prompts

Are you willing to surrender your heart and will to God in order to host His presence?

_____

_____

_____

_____

_____

_____

_____

_____

_____

_____

_____

_____

What intentional efforts can you make to create a space for God's presence in your daily life?

_____

_____

_____

_____

_____

_____

_____

_____

_____

_____

_____

_____

_____

_____

_____

How have you experienced the power and glory of God's presence in your own life and environment?

_____

_____

_____

_____

_____

_____

_____

_____

_____

_____

_____

_____

_____

_____

_____

Are you willing to accept the blessings and challenges that come with hosting God's presence?

_____

_____

_____

_____

_____

_____

_____

_____

_____

_____

_____

_____

_____

How can you cultivate a lifestyle of holiness and righteousness in order to better host God's presence?

_____

_____

_____

_____

_____

_____

_____

_____

_____

_____

_____

_____

_____

_____

_____

In what areas of your life do you need to repent and ask God to purge any impurities or sin?

_____

_____

_____

_____

_____

_____

_____

_____

_____

_____

_____

_____

_____

_____

_____

Are you open to experiencing God's presence in any moment and any place, even outside of traditional church settings?

_____

_____

_____

_____

_____

_____

_____

_____

_____

_____

_____

_____

_____

_____

The One Key to Walking in Authority

Key Lessons

1. Walking in authority requires a relationship with God through Jesus Christ, and it is the only way to access the power and authority of the third heaven.

2. Faith in God's Word is essential to walking in authority, and believers must have a deep understanding of the truth of God's Word to live in authority.

3. Obedience to God's commands is necessary for walking in authority, and believers must be willing to surrender their own will to God's will.

4. Humility is key to walking in authority, as it requires acknowledging that our own strength is insufficient and relying on God's strength.

5. Walking in authority requires a willingness to confront the forces of darkness, and believers must be prepared to engage in spiritual warfare to overcome them.

Action Prompts

How strong is your relationship with God through Jesus Christ?

_____

_____

_____

_____

_____

_____

_____

_____

_____

_____

_____

_____

_____

Do you have a deep understanding of the truth of God's Word?

_____

_____

_____

_____

_____

_____

_____

_____

_____

_____

_____

_____

_____

_____

How willing are you to surrender your own will to God's will?

_____

_____

_____

_____

_____

_____

_____

_____

_____

_____

_____

_____

_____

_____

How humble are you in your walk with God?

_____

_____

_____

_____

_____

_____

_____

_____

_____

_____

_____

_____

_____

_____

Are you prepared to engage in spiritual warfare to overcome the forces of darkness?

_____

_____

_____

_____

_____

_____

_____

_____

_____

_____

_____

_____

_____

_____

_____

_____

How do you cultivate faith in God's Word?

_____

_____

_____

_____

_____

_____

_____

_____

_____

_____

_____

_____

_____

_____

_____

What steps can you take to strengthen your relationship with God and walk in greater authority?

_____

_____

_____

_____

_____

_____

_____

_____

_____

_____

_____

_____

_____

_____

How to Keep Your Faith Strong

Key Lessons

1. Keep your focus on God and His Word, not on circumstances or feelings, to maintain strong faith.

2. Choose to speak God's Word over your life and circumstances, and refuse to speak negative words.

3. Stay connected to God through prayer, worship, and fellowship with other believers.

4. Develop a strong foundation of biblical knowledge and understanding to strengthen your faith.

5. Endure trials and challenges by persevering in faith and trusting in God's faithfulness and goodness.

Action Prompts

In what ways do you allow your circumstances or feelings to dictate your level of faith?

_____

_____

_____

_____

_____

_____

_____

_____

_____

_____

_____

_____

_____

_____

How often do you speak negative words over your life and circumstances? What steps can you take to change this habit?

_____

_____

_____

_____

_____

_____

_____

_____

_____

_____

_____

_____

_____

_____

How consistent are you in your prayer, worship, and fellowship with other believers?

_____

_____

_____

_____

_____

_____

_____

_____

_____

_____

_____

_____

_____

_____

_____

How much time do you devote to studying and
understanding the Bible? How can you prioritize this in
your daily life?

_____

_____

_____

_____

_____

_____

_____

_____

_____

_____

_____

_____

_____

What challenges have you faced in your faith journey,
and how have you persevered through them?

_____

_____

_____

_____

_____

_____

_____

_____

_____

_____

_____

_____

_____

_____

_____

How do you view God's faithfulness and goodness, and how does this affect your faith?

_____

_____

_____

_____

_____

_____

_____

_____

_____

_____

_____

_____

_____

_____

What steps can you take to strengthen your faith and
deepen your relationship with God?

_____

_____

_____

_____

_____

_____

_____

_____

_____

_____

_____

_____

_____

The Pillars of Third-Heaven Authority

Key Lessons

1. The first pillar of third-heaven authority is faith, which is a supernatural substance that brings the promises of God into reality.

2. The second pillar is righteousness, which involves living a life that is pleasing to God and aligning one's will with His.

3. The third pillar is the power of the blood of Jesus, which has the power to cleanse us from sin and grant us access to the third heaven.

4. The fourth pillar is prayer, which is a powerful tool for accessing the third heaven and waging spiritual warfare against the enemy.

5. The fifth pillar is worship, which opens the door to the third heaven and allows us to experience the presence and power of God.

Action Prompts

In what ways have you seen your faith bring the promises of God into reality?

_____

_____

_____

_____

_____

_____

_____

_____

_____

_____

_____

_____

_____

How can you align your will with God's and live a life of righteousness?

_____

_____

_____

_____

_____

_____

_____

_____

_____

_____

_____

_____

_____

_____

_____

Have you fully embraced the power of the blood of Jesus and its ability to cleanse you from sin?

_____

_____

_____

_____

_____

_____

_____

_____

_____

_____

_____

_____

_____

How can you deepen your prayer life and use it to access the third heaven and fight spiritual battles?

_____

_____

_____

_____

_____

_____

_____

_____

_____

_____

_____

_____

Are you prioritizing worship as a means of experiencing the presence and power of God? How are you doing it?

_____

_____

_____

_____

_____

_____

_____

_____

_____

_____

_____

_____

_____

_____

Which of the five pillars do you feel strongest in, and which do you need to work on?

_____

_____

_____

_____

_____

_____

_____

_____

_____

_____

_____

_____

_____

_____

How can you integrate these pillars into your daily life and walk with God?

_____

_____

_____

_____

_____

_____

_____

_____

_____

_____

_____

_____

_____

Learning Review Questions

What made you purchase this workbook?

_____

_____

_____

_____

_____

_____

How have you been using the workbook so far?

_____

_____

_____

_____

_____

_____

What do you feel you have gained from using the workbook?

_____

_____

_____

_____

_____

_____

How has the workbook helped you to achieve your goals?

_____

_____

_____

_____

_____

_____

_____

Are there any parts of the workbook that were particularly helpful or challenging for you?

_____

_____

_____

_____

_____

_____

How has your understanding or knowledge of the topic changed since working through the workbook?

_____

_____

_____

_____

_____

_____

_____

How do you plan to continue using the workbook or incorporating the information in your life?

_____

_____

_____

_____

_____

_____

_____

Made in United States
Troutdale, OR
08/04/2023